THE STAIRWAY TO SUCCESS
STANDS BEFORE YOU.

It promises to transform those who climb it
into happier, richer, more fulfilled people.
It beckons to you.
Are *you* ready to climb it?

"Dear Fellow Traveler, only men and angels can
change themselves from beautiful to ugly. Choose
beauty. Choose caring. Choose love. There is a
stairway that contains the eight essential steps
to successful living. Follow this path and you will
find your true identity. You will take your place
among God's greatest creatures."

—*Frederick Carter*

Steps on the Stairway

BY
RALPH RANSOM

BANTAM BOOKS
TORONTO · NEW YORK · LONDON · SYDNEY

*This low-priced Bantam Book
has been completely reset in a type face
designed for easy reading, and was printed
from new plates. It contains the complete
text of the original hard-cover edition.*
NOT ONE WORD HAS BEEN OMITTED.

STEPS ON THE STAIRWAY

*A Bantam Book / published by arrangement with
Frederick Fell Publishers, Inc.*

PRINTING HISTORY

Frederick Fell edition published August 1982

Bantam edition / April 1983

ISBN 0-553-23196-0

Published simultaneously in the United States and Canada

PRINTED IN THE UNITED STATES OF AMERICA

O   0 9 8 7 6 5 4 3 2 1

This book is dedicated
with deep affection
to my family,
Roy, Ella, Champe, Mary and Jane,
whose love and encouragement I cherish so much,
and
to all who have touched my life,
for they are now a part of my destiny,
a part of my journey to God.

Contents

Your True Identity 1
The Hour of Eight 5
The Good Ground 11

The First Step: **Learning to Listen** 19
The Second Step: **To Struggle** 31
The Third Step: **Learning to Give** 41
The Fourth Step: **Use of Failure** 51
The Fifth Step: **Be a Doer** 61
The Sixth Step: **Thankfulness** 71
The Seventh Step: **Respect** 81
The Eighth Step: **Self-Motivation** 91

The Treasure 103
The Plan 109
A Farewell 115

Your True Identity

WHO are you?

You came into this world as one of God's greatest creatures.

What have you done to yourself? What have you chosen to become?

The answer to these questions contains your destiny.

A small number of our kindred have chosen to walk the light-filled path of caring and progress. Their name is creator.

Many of our brothers and sisters have chosen to be slaves of the subhuman world of violence, hatred and mediocrity. Their name is destroyer.

On your journey notice this truth: Not what happens to a man but how he uses what happens to him is the key to a successful life. The sun shines on everyone. The rains fall on the good and the bad. Sickness and health, failure and new beginnings come to us all. Those who understand this mystery know the ingredients of happiness. They have the courage to choose life and speak a beautiful new language.

They say to us, "God loves me. I am very beautiful. God made me to be truly happy. I have many brothers and sisters in my family. The world is a precious garden God gave my family to care for and to cultivate. All my brothers and sisters must share with me in the fruits of this garden. Our happiness and our destiny are intertwined."

Dear Fellow Traveler, only men and angels can change themselves from beautiful to ugly. Choose beauty. Choose caring. Choose love. There is a mysterious stairway that contains the eight essential steps to successful living. Follow this path and you will find your true identity. You will take your place among God's greatest creatures.

Let me tell my story.

The Hour of Eight

FREDERICK CARTER could sense that the time had come. He had spent eight years planning for this moment. He moved his lean body back easily in the lounge chair and peered intently at the six men and three women who sat before him. Eight of them possessed the necessary steps for successful living and the other had the power to reveal these secrets to the world.

For Frederick this was a sacred moment whose time had come and he was savoring the last few moments of anticipation before he called the gathering to order.

Eight years ago Frederick Carter retired from the company he had founded and had brought to organizational and financial maturity. He and his wife Sarah had planned together many restful years away from the pressures of the company. There would be plenty of time to seriously consider how to recycle the numerous blessings they had received during life. But Sarah's early death had brought the wall tumbling down. She was the love of his life, his inspiration, his intimate advisor. Now she was gone. So much they had planned to share together during the twilight of their lives. It was as though half of his life were gone.

Carter's thoughts were those of sorrow mingled with pleasant memories as he sat quietly in the presence of his guests. The wonderful future he and Sarah planned had come to an abrupt end. Now all his concentration must focus on the second goal of his retirement. He remembered how hard it was at first. He missed her so much and it was easy to drift back into moments of sadness and self-pity. But Frederick Carter was determined to accomplish what they had planned to do together, alone. It had become a daily occupation. How would he recycle the remainder of his wealth? Would it be a hospital, a foundation to help the arts, scholarships to the needy and talented? If only he had Sarah with him, the joy of working on the questions together would have brought him such great happiness. But finally the answer had come. What was it his wife had said so often? "Learn from the great and the good. Enrich others with what you have received." A smile slowly lit up the old man's face. How obvious it was. Sarah had the answer to the problem all the time, she only wanted him to see it for himself. Her death was a seed planting and he was going to bring in the first harvest. Surely the answer had not come easily or quickly or even crystal clear for a number of years.

But once Frederick saw the answer he bent all his energies toward bringing the plan into action.

Great and good men and women had the real treasures he wanted to recycle. They were hidden in all walks of life. Frederick had traveled widely during his business years and it was only a matter of carefully selecting those who best exemplified the path to true'success. He already knew the men and women he wanted to take part in his plan, if only they would be willing to publicly cooperate in his final adventure. Tonight they sat before him.

For one week the group had been his guests and slowly they had become a family. They were comfortable and open in each other's presence. As host, Frederick had decided the order in which they were to speak and share their secrets of success. Each guest embodied to some degree the eight essential steps to successful living but each would speak on the topic his life most revealed. Frederick looked at his watch, and although his company was enjoying themselves in spirited conversation, the hour was eight in the evening and it was time to begin.

The Good Ground

MY dear friends, during the last few days we have become a family of loving friends. You have brought me much joy and happiness these hours we have spent together. Our mutual love and respect is the way the human family should always live. As you know, for the past few years I have bent all my energies to discovering the necessary ingredients to successful living. In my studies I have found that there are eight essential steps to success. You are the flesh and blood examples of my findings and soon you will get the chance to share with each other the beautiful secrets of your lives.

"But for now let an old man ramble for a while. As I speak I will be talking to myself, talking to you and talking to unseen men and women who are in my mind's eye. I know you have prepared your presentations well, but what I say now is most necessary if the eight steps of the stairway are to bear fruit. A great stillness pervaded the room.

"Life is a series of steps. Things are done gradually. Every once in a while there is a giant step, but most of the time we are taking small, seemingly insignificant steps on the stairway of life. If we are not climbing the stairway, our lives are hollow and aimless. But if we walk—one step at a time—always climbing, wonderful changes begin to take place within us.

"There are eight necessary steps on the stairway of life. They are the eight essential steps to success. They are the building blocks of life. Life is like a mirror. You frown at it, it glares back at you; you smile at life and it returns the smile. Thus as you will to become better, as you will to change, as you fill your mind and imagination with great thoughts and ideals, you are preparing the soil of your life for success. Life becomes what you think about, imagine, plan and act on.

"But the ground of my life is hard. Like the farmer's field, it needs to be loosened. I need to get out the tiller and the plow. The field of my mind and heart lay sleeping. The ground is hard and rocky, unattended and unsown. I must get rid of the hard and barren field. God has destined the soil of my life to be flexible, a soil that can be made into rows for planting. I want good ground that can accept the seed and yield a harvest. I will till the soil and like the farmer I will work the ground. I will constantly be preparing the earth of my being to produce good fruit.

"The ground needs water, minerals and sunshine. So does my mind and heart. The sunshine of good thoughts, the minerals of positive ideas and rainwater to keep my mind open and alive. Yet how often I starve myself for lack of these precious ingredients. If I want good ground, I will see to it that the ground of my being is watered and fed. To nourish my mind and will is so important that I will make it as natural as breathing. It will become my life, because I want good ground. I want to yield a harvest of my full potential—first ten fold, then thirty fold and someday a hundred fold.

"I must work each day to make the soil productive. As surely as the sun rises gloriously in the east and sets each day gently in the west I will be at work on the ground of my soul. The key is: daily. It is only the persevering worker who eventually obtains the prize. Those who work for a time and then fall by the wayside will never claim the harvest. Those who start tilling the soil but then wander off after an easy life are not worthy of success. They will not succeed. The man who puts his hand to the plow and then glances back will not gain the harvest. We never know exactly when the harvest will come or how bountiful it will be, but we do know that to receive the riches of the earth we must continue each day to feed our field with sunshine, water and minerals.

"The seed I plant must be good seed. My harvest depends on it. What I sow, I will reap. I will look everywhere for good seed. I will plant the best seed I can find. No price is too great to pay for the seed that will yield the harvest that I desire. The search for good seed will fill the days of my life. How foolish is the man who plants inferior seed in his garden. His life will be a constant reaping of inferior produce. Life is too short to waste time on a mediocre harvest. I want to fill my land with all the beauty, all the restful shade and all the sweet-tasting fruit that comes only from planting good seed. If what I sow is what I will reap, I will sow only the best.

"Weeds are not to be a part of my garden. I will root out the weeds that clutter the field of my life. The weeds of hatred and selfishness I will remove. I will do away with all those lazy and destructive habits that take energy and life from the ground. Just as I plant day by day, so will I remove the weeds. The loveliness and total yield of my garden demands it. Weeds steal from me. They take away beauty and taste from the grapes of my vineyard. I will not allow them to suck away precious goodness from the delicious wine of my life.

"The success of the farmer depends on his ground; that is why its condition is so important to him. He needs and thanks God for the rays of the sun. He needs and thanks God for the gentle rains. He works long hours by the sweat of his brow to fertilize and replenish the minerals in his land. I need to do the same. The land of my mind is more important than the land of the farmer. His soil produces a food to nourish physical life. My soil is my very life. I must have good soil.

"Things grow on good ground. The good ground is lovely. There are beautiful trees and flowers. The fruits from the trees and the plants give nourishment and life. Everywhere you look, the eye beholds the goodness of life. The air is touched with the pleasant fragrance of fresh blossoms. All is good. All is as God intended it. Why? Because the seed was planted on good ground. Learn this all-important first lesson. You must plant good seed and you must plant it on good ground. Nothing grows on the parched land. Nothing can survive on land covered with weeds and thistles. It will choke and die. Nothing comes forth from hard and rocky ground. Look to the seed you plant and the ground you plant it on and you will discover the secret of each man's success and the reason for his defeats.

"The good ground will make you rich. Un-dreamed-of wealth comes to the man who plants on land with a good top soil. Do you want to bring to the marketplace valuable sought-after goods? Picture in your mind a medium-sized plantation. On the northern hills a beautiful vineyard is planted with the grapes glistening in the morning sun. To the south many head of cattle graze on a lush carpet of grass. To the west a restful lake filled with fish and white-breasted ducks gliding along the surface. To the east stands an attractive country home surrounded by acres of neatly planted crops. Look again and see the house landscaped by shade trees and a brilliant array of flowers. See the beige-coated mare and the frisky colt. All blend together, producing for the owner deep satisfaction and a more than adequate income. This plantation can be mine and yours because planting good seed on good ground makes you richer than you ever dreamed possible.

"My friends, look how the good ground helps others. A farmer does not plant just for himself. His daily work reaches far past himself and the members of his family. His hours of toil feed many people he will never see or meet. You can never just enrich yourself. Sowing on the good ground reaches out farther and farther, touching more and more people. The old saying that you can't get to heaven alone rings true; you have to bring someone with you. The soil on which I plant yields a shared product. The adventure of life is to always get better. The deepest joy of life is to always enrich others. Man's calling is to produce a great human being made in the image and likeness of God. This is the only calling worthy of his nature. As I grow, others must benefit from my growth. My harvest passes on a satisfaction that never runs dry.

"Life's work is to prepare the ground on which the seed will fall. Now I shall put my hand to the plow and begin producing the good ground. Now it is time to begin revealing the eight steps of the stairway. Each day is an image of my life. I will learn how to make every day a better day, a more glorious and productive day. Learning the eight steps to successful living will ennoble my present life and be my hope for the future. I will begin to practice the eight secrets that have produced all the great men and women who have ever lived.

"My dear brothers and sisters, each one of us is already on the stairway of life, our only life on this earth. If we hold true to the great calling that has been given to us and make the eight steps of the stairway our way of life, then we can climb forever as the eagle who soars high into the heavens."

Tears were in the old man's eyes as he nodded to the first speaker.

1

Learning to Listen

ROY BLAISE edged forward in his chair. He knew that he was the first speaker. Roy was a muscular man but the first impression you got was not one of muscle and bodily strength but of self-confidence, a man at peace with himself. You could tell right away that he enjoyed your company and was interested in you. For the past twenty-two years he had been a very successful high school coach and school counselor. Dedication to his work and a love for young people had filled his years with happiness and a deep sense of fulfillment. Roy was anxious to begin and when he got the nod from Mr. Carter he eased gently into his talk. "Ladies and gentlemen . . .

"A few years ago I met a gentleman whom I have admired from a distance since early childhood. As the years passed I often thought about the ingredients that went into the 'final' product of what this man is today. Many things came to mind: his early environment, his happy outlook on life, the willingness to think big, the courage to pay the price and the many other qualities that help develop a great person. But it wasn't until we came face to face that I finally realized the basic ingredient of this wonderful human being's success. He knew how to listen.

"The first step on the stairway is learning to listen. This is the first essential ingredient of living successfully. Few know this truth, fewer still follow its wisdom. The wise man listens, the fool talks. This first step on the stairway of life is so important, but so neglected. Yet your future progress depends on it. The ancient philosopher Epictetus once wrote:

> Nature has given to men one tongue, but two ears, that we may hear from others twice as much as we speak.

Most people talk too much, they don't know how to listen. When you seriously study the truly great men and women of history you will notice one basic quality: They had the marvelous ability of knowing how to listen.

"There is nothing more difficult to learn. There is nothing harder to do. But there is nothing more essential than learning to listen. Listening is not just being quiet and hearing—that is the first step, and hard enough in itself. Listening is soaking up not only the words of the speaker, but his point of view, his true feelings, what he is saying beneath the words. Gus Wilhelmy, the director of Challenge, a program for the rehabilitation of former prisoners, writes:

> To receive another is to listen and allow that person to enter one's being, one's emotions, one's thoughts, one's consciousness. In this is creation: the moment of the greatest pain and growth.

When people start listening to one another, miracles begin to take place.

"Just as we have to think to grow, we have to listen to grow. If you find yourself always talking but never listening there is a basic flaw in your journey toward maturity. Greatness demands silence. Greatness demands listening. The first step toward greatness of soul is learning to listen. 'Until a man has learned to listen he has no right to speak.'

"Before we can convince ourselves that we should stop talking so much and hear from others, we have a difficult task to perform. We will never learn to listen, we will never even want to listen until we are deeply convinced that the other person has something worthwhile to say. If we are not convinced of this we will have no desire or motivating force drawing us toward the habit of listening. We must have a genuine and deep-seated belief that every man and woman we meet has something important to say. It may take a while, it may take some doing on our part to get off the chitchat stage, but every man can teach us. Every man has gone through different experiences, moments of joy, bitter suffering, travel, new insights and a thou-

sand other life events. Others can teach us if only
we will give each one his due and our reward—
listen to him.

"Listening sets the stage whereby we can learn.
It sets an atmosphere whereby another person begins to open up to us the treasures of his life. As I
learn to listen, as I begin to see its value, as I
prepare a listening atmosphere when I meet others, then I am taking an upward step on the stairway of life. My listening attitude is placing me on
the stairway of successful living. It is placing me
in a position to acquire a great amount of personal
happiness.

"At first all conversation may seem petty, vain
and useless. But as we learn to listen and how to
listen, gems of wisdom and new insights appear.
There is no more valuable gift than that of being a
good listener. The wise man acquires the enriching habit of good listening and truly understands
what he hears.

"There is a great false pride in feeling that we
know everything or that our opinion is always the
right one. I say that I am not like that. Then I
must look to how much I talk and how often I
listen. The sign of a know-it-all, the sign of a fool,
is to be always talking. The sign of a mature man
is to have a balance between talking and listening.
Wise old Benjamin Franklin once wrote:

> Better to be silent and let others wonder if
> you are a fool than open your mouth and
> remove all doubt.

"The false pride of not listening says in effect
'I have all the answers' when most of the time we

don't even know the question. Our attitude tells others that as far as we are concerned they are nobodies. The words of scripture point out this dangerous attitude very clearly, 'What good can come out of Nazareth?' The false pride of not being willing to listen is a worse handicap than being deaf or blind. It is an attitude that allows us to bypass the wisdom of the ages and the riches of life. The frightening part is that our false pride gets worse as the years go on. It becomes a blind spot that we never even notice. But we do pay for it. We come up empty-handed instead of finding a treasure. The ideas, suggestions and information that was to be ours is lost forever.

"Often we know that the person before us did not have the advantages of education that we did. They did not have the opportunities of environment. Often true. This very fact could well be the main reason I should listen. In listening I am not looking for yes-men or someone to reinforce my views. I am looking for a new insight. A fresh approach. The invigorating wisdom of common sense. Listen to learn, not to be pacified.

"Learning to listen builds bridges. It allows us to communicate. The great missing ingredient in living a successful life is the ability to communicate. You can never communicate until you have learned how to listen. How often is a marriage ruined? A friendship weakened? An organization made ineffective? Because people are unwilling to listen. Many times while a person is talking we are preparing our arguments against what he is saying, instead of trying to understand what he is saying and why.

"Greatness comes from learning to be attentive to the ideas, opinions and beliefs of others. Many of my fellow travelers on the stairway of life are not climbing, they are not leaders, they are not successful. They often have no desire for greatness. They are deep in the mire of self-pity. Their lives are stagnant with mediocrity. How can I learn from someone like this? Certainly we must have the courage to bid good-bye to the chronic complainer, the negative thinker, the small-talk artist. But you never know what might trigger off a great idea, a new insight. Time and time again, paying attention to what others have to say pays off in rich dividends.

"The successful man listens. This is the difference between an achiever and an excuse giver. The excuse giver is too self-centered to learn from others. When others speak, he shuts them out or listens in a halfhearted manner. Not so the successful man. He becomes absorbed in the conversation, he is always drawing out of the conversation valuable pieces of information that help him reach his goals. He accepts the gifts of the gift giver.

"A few summers ago I was to attend a four-day self-renewal conference in Houston, Texas. Because of the speakers listed, I was convinced that my week would be wasted. Before making the journey to Houston, I made up my mind that I was going to listen very attentively and get something of value from each speaker. As I had expected, the announced speakers were dull and in some cases ill-prepared. But to my amazement I got something valuable out of each presentation. In fact I latched on to two ideas that have had a great influence on my life and will continue to do so. Gems are everywhere but you must look for them.

Good ideas are in the most unexpected places. Learn to listen and you will grow rich.

"The greatest benefit of listening is that it teaches us to know ourselves. Through the years we develop disastrous personality traits. Bad habits take such a hold that we don't even notice them. But others do. Listen to what they have to say. The non-listener becomes the prosecutor, jury and judge of his life. He is not open to ideas or criticism. He decides all things with only half the facts. The fool chooses himself for a lawyer. How much better to listen and discover who you really are.

"Those in positions of authority fail miserably when it comes to listening. They lack real leadership. They feel they don't need to listen to anybody and don't. Things are done without prior consultation or seeking of advice. They may go through the motions of consulting others or forming advisory boards but most of their plans are already an accomplished fact. How small and petty! How disastrous to their personality, to the business they manage and to the customers they are supposed to serve. How proud and selfish! Learn to really listen. Learn to look forward to listening before you chart a course of action. Two minds are better than one. The non-listener invites the bitter sting of defeat. The listener lets wisdom shine through, inviting the sweet touch of victory.

"We have to learn how to listen, it doesn't come automatically. First, you must see the value in listening. Second, you must learn how to set an atmosphere for listening. Without these ingredients you will never become a good listener. Once you see the great value in listening, then you must

consciously set an atmosphere for listening with
every person you meet. Let them know by your
attitude, by not constantly interrupting them, that
you are interested in what they have to say and
you are truly interested in their ideas and viewpoint. You can still steer the conversation toward
ever more enriching topics, but you always remain
the good listener.

"The treasure of listening is unlimited. Its value
is priceless. You are talking with a person at the
mid-point of his life, say the middle forties. What
a treasure! His native culture. His dress. The music
he likes. His favorite foods. Customs. His special
way of looking at things. Maybe years of travel.
Perhaps a great knowledge of the local area. What
about hobbies? Special interests. A younger person will have one approach to life, a senior citizen
an altogether different view. Variety abounds. Personal viewpoint. Cultural background. All these
and many more. What a gold mine!

"Listening changes your personality. It makes
you a better person. Listening helps you to grow.
It teaches you patience. It makes you a better
communicator. It makes you more sensitive, open
and fully human. Listening teaches self-discipline.
It prepares you for the moment when you do speak.
Then your words and thoughts will be more mean-
ingful, more respected, more helpful. The listener
is constantly enriching himself, so he has more to
give when it is time to speak. New insights. A
wider viewpoint. Patience. More sensitivity. A better communicator. These are the trademarks of
greatness.

"You listen when you read. Don't just read
books, READ PEOPLE. This is what you are doing

when you listen to them. You expose yourself to the adventure, knowledge, romance and courage of their lives. As there is great profit in your daily reading, there is great value in your daily listening.

"Catch yourself if you find that you are doing all the talking. Try to draw someone else into the conversation. Are you listening? Are you interested? Begin to get your companion to talk about himself, his experiences, his line of work or business, his travels. Go deeper. Create an atmosphere that encourages the other person to talk, to tell you about himself. Are you listening closely enough to see if the words are not hiding something else he really wants to say? Is he saying one thing but meaning another? Become deeply interested in people. Be quiet and let them give you, free of charge, riches that you may never be able to experience personally.

"Many of the relationships of parent and child, teacher and student, coach and athlete, employers and workers are based on the ability of both parties to listen and understand. All of life is based on good listening. The wise person listens, learns and then goes into action. But the first step is always listening. Leave it out and you aren't on the stairway leading to success, you are in the quagmire leading to failure. So few understand this. Their lives have become a series of disasters, a showcase of mediocrity. All because they did not know the first step of the stairway. Thomas Merton writes in *Thoughts in Solitude*,

> My life is a listening, His is a speaking. My salvation is to hear and respond. For this, my life must be silent. Hence, my silence is my salvation.

"Listening is a sign of true love. It is needed between husband and wife. Between parent and child. Between brother and sister. Between you and every person you meet. The greatest sign that a person loves and respects you is that he listens to the words you speak. These words formed by human sounds express you, the inner mystery of your being. The true lover catches them in all their significance and meaning. He is always searching to move from the utterance of the word to the reality it expresses. Those who learn to listen learn to love.

"In all of life, thousands of opportunities surround us. Every day great treasures come and go unseen by most men. We must prepare to receive the golden seed that will one day bear a great harvest. The first step is learning to listen and in listening, learning to understand. This is the highest of all wisdom. Listening slowly brings about those internal changes and attitudes that are needed before we can allow the riches of life to become a part of our life. Stop throwing away the life-bearing seed that others are offering. Learn to listen and become rich.

Until a man has learned to listen, he has no business teaching: Until he realizes that every man has something of truth and wisdom to offer, he does not begin to learn. It is only when he sees how each of his fellows surpasses him that a man begins to be wise, to himself and to his fellow men."

2

To Struggle

FOR as long as John Ortego could remember he had been picking other people's crops. You don't get much formal education as a Texas migrant farm worker but he was self-educated and a true discerner of people. John could recognize a phony a mile away. His rough, calloused hands and deep brown body gave him a distinctive appearance. He was an outdoor man, a modern-day John the Baptist, a New Testament prophet. Now in his mid-forties he was the leader of the farm workers in the Texas Valley. Step by step he was leading them to new-found freedom and a sense of personal dignity.

Frederick Carter smiled at his weather-beaten friend. This was the signal to reveal another step on the stairway.

"All life demands struggle. Those who have everything given to them become lazy, selfish and insensitive to the real values of life. The very striving and hard work that we so constantly try to avoid is the major building block in the person we are today. My friends, the second step on the stairway of successful living is learning to struggle.

"Too often we try to get something for nothing. We want to get through life without paying the price. How many students seldom study, but at exam time rely on the instant absorption of cramming? How many adults have stopped reading and developing their skills? How many people never really learn their jobs, never ask questions, don't know their line of work? How many professional people—doctors, lawyers, ministers—rely solely on the training they received many years ago in school but do not keep pace with their field of endeavor. We have become a people who take the easy way out. We don't demand anything of ourselves. We don't struggle to draw out more of the latent potential that God placed in the innermost recesses of our being.

"When you leave struggle out of your life you begin to weaken, you begin to shrink from hard work. You start to do only what is asked of you and this many times in a grudging and lackadaisical manner. We begin to think that we have to start at the top and not work our way up. Our whole character begins to deteriorate. The status quo becomes acceptable. We can overlook sloppy work and waste of time becomes a pattern of action. We start to say 'let Harry do it,' instead of 'it needs to be done, I'll do it.'

"Struggle is so essential; there is no growth or

progress without it. Things just don't happen, we make them happen. Those who wait on chance or luck wait their lifetime away. Unless we put our shoulders to the plow, unless we pay the price, we don't really grow and nothing gets done in our lives. 'They fail, and they alone, who have not striven.' Power never yields without a struggle. Every minority group, every person trying to change a long-established system, everyone trying to improve city government soon finds this out. All of history attests to this. To live and make progress is to struggle, strive and then struggle some more.

"If you want to make something of yourself you must understand the secret of the second step on the stairway: Without struggle there is no progress, no greatness, no making of things to happen. To grasp this principle is to grasp life. Struggle is a law so basic to building a better person, so fundamental to building a better world that it is amazing how few people know its value. Before the reward there must be the labor. You plant before you harvest. You sow in tears before you reap in joy.

"I don't like to struggle. I often flinch and hide. But until the day that the principle of struggle becomes an integral part of my life, I will not be able to prosper. I must see the all-important relationship between struggle and progress. It is one of the essential ingredients of a truly successful life. The longer I put off applying this principle, the longer I am putting off the day of my success. The great destiny that could be mine calls for a deep commitment to daily struggle. Man was made in such a way that to reach a goal he must work and he must work hard—he must struggle.

"Struggle in its highest form is not climbing on other men's shoulders and pushing them down so you can get ahead. It is not even, in its best sense, competing with others, trying to be better than they are. Struggle is competing with yourself. It is trying to use and develop every fiber of your potential. Struggle demands that the system—institutions, governments, cultures—give you the freedom you need to realize your greatness. Often we have to struggle against the system itself because it denies us growth and opportunity. But the basic struggle is always within us. It is that constant warfare to rid ourselves of all that holds us back from becoming the wonderful person God created us to be. Struggle is the ingredient that makes men great. It is the indispensable attitude that is needed on every step of the stairway. Read carefully the words of Frederick Douglass.

IF THERE IS NO STRUGGLE,
THERE IS NO PROGRESS.
THOSE WHO PROFESS TO FAVOR FREEDOM,
AND YET DEPRECATE AGITATION,
ARE MEN WHO WANT CROPS
WITHOUT PLOWING UP THE GROUND.
THEY WANT RAIN
WITHOUT THUNDER AND LIGHTNING.
THEY WANT THE OCEAN
WITHOUT THE AWFUL ROAR OF ITS MANY WATERS.
POWERS CONCEDES NOTHING WITHOUT A DEMAND.

"The words Mr. Douglass wrote describe what is necessary if we really want something. Whatever the odds, you will obtain a victory if you don't give up. Look at the amazing work the entertainer, Jerry Lewis, has accomplished with his annual Muscular Dystrophy Telethon. He saw something that needed to be done, something he really believed in. His efforts have brought about a modern miracle and people were encouraged to respond to his dream. Andrew Jackson once said that 'one man with courage is a majority.' The great lesson of struggle is that you develop yourself, you develop your inner powers. Out of struggle comes victory. Victory belongs to the men and women of this world who never quit trying, who never give up. Harriet Beecher Stowe said it well, 'When you get into a tight place and everything goes against you, till it seems as though you could not hold on a minute longer, never give up then, for that is just the place and time that the tide will turn.'

"All great events demand struggle. A people striving to be free, a research team working on a cure for some mysterious disease. Every worthwhile endeavor succeeds only after years of hard work. Read the famous chapters on Thomas Edison and his co-workers in the invention of the electric light bulb. Study carefully the history of the building of the Panama Canal.

"Struggle means to put forth great efforts, to labor hard, to strive. It is not just the ordinary way of approaching life. There is time for recreation, time for fun, but there is a time for work.

"Many people let life pass by without putting their best into it. A job well done is its own reward. All advancement means struggle. For those who wish to succeed it is the battle cry of life. Each day we enter anew into the struggle of developing the best that is within us, of doing the best job we can, of walking the extra mile. We don't have to have someone looking over our shoulder begging us to do our best. The mature man or woman doesn't need a fawning crowd applauding them on. Our struggles have a higher motivation—to realize that great potential that lies buried deep within us.

"Struggle produces results. It helps recreate the world in which we live. Any organization that is succeeding indicates that there are some people hard at work making the wheels turn. If you find a good school, an aggressive club, a spirit-filled church, then you know efforts are being put forth and struggle is taking place.

"Struggle produces interior results. The best results always take place within us. Who can place a true value on the growth in faith that struggle brings? Struggle develops the power of perseverance, the inner qualities of self-confidence and self-discipline. You have to pay the price for an object of great value. Man grows from within. The person who has learned how to struggle is setting in motion an interior growth that endures. No event worthy of greatness comes without a struggle. The greatest struggle of all is the struggle that goes on within a man. The struggle begins when he starts to seek greatness. Words cannot describe the tug of war that rages within a human being when the spirit wants to grow and develop. The lazy, the easy-way-out man, the satisfied, the don't-rock-the-boat thinker, they do not know what I am talking about. But those who have chosen to climb the stairway know that struggle is the key to success.

"A person who is willing to work for something reveals his true interests and values. If we lack struggle in our lives this is a sign that our goals and priorities have not been properly set. There is struggle in just the art of survival but what we strive for lets us know our real values. Struggle is the mirror on the wall telling us who we are and what we want to be.

"Don't look for something for nothing. Pay the price. Struggle is a healthy ingredient that should be a part of every man's life. Never let other people, by their remarks or actions, sway you from the principle of struggle. Many people become very jealous and guilt-ridden when they see someone trying to improve. Many people become very upset when someone tries to do a better job or change an 'accepted' injustice. The second step on the stairway is to know that if there is no struggle, there is no progress. Robert Louis Stevenson said it very well in the *Spires of El Dorado*, 'true success is to labor.' We begin to succeed when we start working on it. Progress demands a struggle.

NOTHING IN THE WORLD
CAN TAKE THE PLACE
OF PERSISTENCE. TALENT WILL NOT;
NOTHING IS MORE COMMON THAN
UNSUCCESSFUL MEN WITH TALENT.
GENIUS WILL NOT;
UNREWARDED GENIUS
IS ALMOST A PROVERB.
EDUCATION ALONE WILL NOT;
THE WORLD IS FULL
OF EDUCATED DERELICTS.
PERSISTENCE AND DETERMINATION
ALONE ARE OMNIPOTENT."

Learning to Give

TISH BRYAN was an attractive woman. She was married and had three handsome boys, the youngest now a junior in college. Tish was an accomplished artist but her real love was Opportunity Center, an activity and educational center for retarded children and their families. It was her home away from home. Tish Bryan was instrumental in founding Opportunity Center and she had given of herself in every phase of its development. She was one of those quiet leaders who got a lot accomplished behind the scenes. Her marriage and family life, her work in the local art groups and her generous work at the Center made her well qualified to present the next step on the stairway. Frederick Carter's voice filled the room, "Tish, it is now your turn to develop and explain the next step toward successful living."

"My new-found brothers and sisters, it is more blessed to give than to receive. Test any principle of life that you hold dear and it will contain in some way this idea. This secret key to successful living is a stumbling block to many. For most people it is a hard saying, a bitter contradiction to their way of living. How can it be that if you are trying to get ahead, if you are trying to be a success, you must give? It seems only proper and logical that you would always try to receive and very seldom would you give. This principle, a hidden mystery to so many, is the third essential step on the stairway. It is indeed more blessed to give than to receive.

"Why is there a special blessing in giving? Why do we actually have to give before we are ready to receive? How deeply it is ingrained in most of us that the more you gather to yourself and the less you share, the richer you will become. Many people feel this way. But for true happiness, for true success, for true enrichment, you must give. You must give of your time, your talent and your wealth. The day you stop giving, on that day you stop enriching yourself. When you stop giving, everything you acquire and accumulate, instead of enriching you, will begin to drag you down.

"Shared wealth. That is the phrase I want to use. If you don't or can't share it, it is not worth having. The days, and weeks and years that we slave feverishly to accomplish and accumulate things only for ourselves eventually turn into a hellish nightmare. Share your riches. Share whatever health nature has given your body. Share the mind that you have developed through the years, share the possessions that have come to you by hard work and careful planning. Part of true success is that you have the attitude, the mind and the power to make things better. This world has to be a better place because you are here. Measure your life not only by what you have but also by what you have shared, by what good you have done.

"So many times even when we give we are looking to receive. Don't concentrate on receiving, that will come automatically. But it will not always come perceptibly. It might not always come from the person to whom you gave. Often it comes later. Most times it comes in a way that you least expect and in far greater measure than you anticipated. Remember, don't give to receive—give to share. 'The reward of a good deed is to have done it.'

"Many wealthy people give only to the sure thing, the popular causes, the big tax deductible organizations. There is nothing wrong with this as long as it does not stop here. It is good to call to mind that many of these large, over-organized charitable fund raising groups end up spending 90% of your dollar on administration and 10% or less of your dollar on the cause you intended to help. Expand your sharing. Help a man get into business. Buy a typewriter, mimeograph machine or organ for a small church. Help build a structure that will give years of service to a community—a place of worship, a branch library, a fine arts center or recreation park. The ideas can go on and on in ways that allow you to share your wealth and enrich yourself. Don't be afraid to give big—not

$50, $100, etc. to fifteen diverse causes but $5,000, $50,000 and more to get one job done.

"I have been talking big money, haven't I? Most of us will never get the blessed opportunity to share to that extent. But don't let yourself off the hook. Share of what time, attitude, ability, skill, finances you have. Because the principle stays the same. 'It is more blessed to give than to receive.'

"Many who have been blessed with this world's goods don't share because they are afraid they might make a mistake or as they express it, they might 'be taken.' In the law of averages they will. As in all phases of your development there will be mistakes. But this should never stop anyone from gaining the immense riches that giving will bring to him. We are talking about a whole attitude toward life. An attitude that will make your life really worthwhile. What is at stake here is one of the fundamental and essential ingredients of being a truly great person. Never sacrifice this principle or any other principle because of difficulties or the risk of making a few mistakes. Practice and experience in giving will make you a better and wiser giver. We never really possess anything just for ourselves. God allows us to acquire things, talents and time that we might grow rich by sharing.

"The greatest stumbling block on the stairway is this attitude of giving. Many refuse to allow giving to have a special place in their lives. When they do this they can climb no farther. They stop their journey on the stairway of life. When you stop giving, then you also stop growing, you stop climbing, you stop really living.

"The concept 'It is better to give than to receive,' is a very hard one to understand and

practice, but it is one of the essential ideas in any
system of true self-development. Great people don't
just enrich themselves, they enrich as many people as their talents, time and material blessings
allow.

"Giving forces you to start thinking of the best
way to give. How your giving can be more useful
and effective. At times a gift of time, talent and
finances to a small or little-known group does the
most good. Thus, once you start to give and share
you have to take stock of yourself and ask yourself
what group, what project you should support and
what form your support should take. All of this is
making you a better and better giver.

"Giving makes you realize that what you have
received is not just for yourself. There comes that
moment when you see that what you have received
was meant to be shared. You are an instrument of
God's plan to pass on, in deeds of giving, the blessings you enjoy. It is only when you start giving
that you really come to an indisputable knowledge
that what you have from life must be passed on to
others. Nothing is just for yourself. You have received that you might share.

"Giving helps us to break the unhealthy at-
tachment that we have to the things, opinions and
abilities that are ours. Never be a slave to the
things you have. This great step on the stairway is
meant to make you free. A false security in our
possessions means death to greatness. If you are
possessed by your possessions you are not a free
man.

"Giving is a sign that our true wealth is from
within. A person who has to hoard things to himself or is constantly worried about his material

wealth is very insecure. The truly great man knows that it is not his external wealth that makes him who he is but the inner forces of his being. His greatness comes from within. His security is founded on God and in the deep recesses of the spirit. He is not solely dependent on his wealth. Giving reinforces the fact that our strength is an inner strength.

"We have been helped by the giving of others. Don't think you haven't. There is no such creature as a self-made man. All our self-made men have to do is reflect a little and they will see any number of people who helped them along the way. The author of a book, a teacher, a friend that had faith in them. It is now our turn to help others. Be a giver.

"People who do not give become selfish and the product of selfishness is unhappiness. A person can be surrounded by a multitude of possessions but if they become self-centered and not other-centered, they will be very unhappy. Happiness is not something you strive for directly. It is a by-product of helping others. It is a by-product of loving others. The drinking and drug problems among the rich is alarming. The number of suicides and attempted suicides is great. You are an unhappy person if you can't give and give freely with no strings attached. You are an unhappy person if it hurts you to give.

"A person must eventually account for his wealth just as he must account for his time and talents. Accountability is measured by what you give, what you shared. How we have used the blessings of life is important because we are held responsible for what we have. We can make a good account of our possessions if we learn to give generously.

"As the camp fires of our life burn low we should be able to look back on a life of intense sharing. We must not be remembered for what we have but for what we have given to the family of man. Only a great human being can be a giver. To climb even higher on the stairway we have to be blessed because we generously gave back from the abundance of what we received.

"Don't wait until you die to share. In order for you to grow and mature you must give now. Don't say, 'I don't have enough to share.' Find something to share. Share your time, your skills, help others with advice or by your creative hobbies. Don't let a week go by without being able to look back and see that you have given generously of yourself. This is true greatness. Giving breeds greatness. It is the sign of a great person.

"Deep down in our hearts we all tell ourselves that we will give after we acquire a little more. Once we receive the large salary, win the lucky sweepstake and make the big sale, then certainly we intend to give. Friend, if you are not giving now, you will not give later. We are creatures of habit. If we are stingy, if we are close-fisted while we have little, the same will be true if we have great wealth. People say they would be generous if only they had a lot to spare. If you think you will give when you have a great surplus, be a little suspicious. You will never think you have a great surplus. What you give now, you will give proportionally later.

"Giving is hard. We want to receive and we spend a lot of time in planning and effort to make sure we receive. We put little planning and effort into our program of giving. Giving is like taking a pound of flesh. It hurts. Many people are not ready for this step on the stairway. The maturity and inner growth necessary to be able to give comes slowly and painfully. If you are hurt every time you give, this is a sign that you have a lot of work to do in making this step. Giving is so essential to climbing the stairway that you must develop the pow r to do so. If you lack it, the climb stops. It is an essential ingredient to a great life. It can't be deferred. Give now a portion of what you have or realize that you will never give. You have heard of the phrase, 'the stingy rich.' This applies to some people. Like everyone else, they said in their heart that if they ever got wealthy they would give and help others. But as they got richer and richer they were always waiting for some magical sum of wealth to put them in a position to give. It never came. They never gave of their time, their abilities or their material blessings. By not having a spirit of giving when they had less, they lost the golden opportunity to enrich themselves by giving. They never acquired this inner power of greatness, the power to give. They could not take that step on the stairway that we all so desperately need to take. If my life—and your life—is not a life of giving, it is not really a life at all.

4

Use of Failure

RON SIMON was not a tough off the streets but you could tell he was tough. He had to be. If nothing else, Ron had to be tough mentally because he worked with ex-cons every day of his life. He himself was an ex, not an ex-con but an ex-parole officer and an ex-policeman. But twelve years ago he opened up a halfway house for ex-convicts. He still spent a lot of time on the streets and visiting the jails but he had now found his life's work, to try to reintegrate human beings into a suspicious and two-systemed world. A world that has a different justice for the rich and the poor, the black and the white, the educated and the uneducated. Ron did grow up in a rough neighborhood. He was a fine athlete in school and from his training in the military and police work he

could make his weight felt if need be. But Ron
Simon succeeded in his profession in other ways.
If you are tough you don't have to act tough. If you
really want to help people, the only show you have
to put on is one of sincere concern and dedication
to progress. The lumps of life had not made Ron a
sour man but one who knew the price you had to
pay to make something of yourself. The eyes of
Ron Simon and Frederick Carter met. The fourth
step on the stairway was about to be revealed.

"My friends, the fourth step on the stairway is
our attitude toward failure. I have a hard time
talking objectively about failure because I am so
close to it all the time. We all are. I have failed all
my life. Thus it seems that I may be termed a
failure. Many of us feel very deeply that we are.
We see project after project, opportunity after opportunity where we failed. The evidence stares us
daily in the face. Our marriages. The job. The
things we were going to do in life. So many things.
We expected so much from life and look how it
turned out. So you see, because of our many mistakes and shortcomings it is vital that we have a
proper attitude and understanding of our failures.
We must learn how to use failure, and even growth,
from past and present setbacks.

"One reason for our sense of failure is that our
minds so readily remember our mistakes, misfortunes and shortcomings. We might not be as tall
as we would like to be. Maybe we weigh too much.
We are not as good at sports, conversation or the
art of dancing as others. The list can go on and on.
Each one of us has a number of 'strikes' against us.
How we look, our intelligence, our eyesight. Some
have a debilitating disease, a deformity or a scar.

You name it, we all have things that weigh us down. We all have drawbacks that lead us to experience a sense of failure. Our waste of time. Our selfishness. The minds adds up and concentrates on these things and gives many a man and woman a sense of being a failure. With all these pressures upon us it is no wonder often we have a very low self-esteem.

"You see, the evidence is there. We can't forget the facts. We have failed and failed many times. But now we must have the courage to look deeper. God did not place us on this earth to be failures. Who decides if I am a failure? How do we judge between failure and defeat, success and victory?

"Some thoughts to ponder. First of all, when we say the word failure, as in 'I am a failure,' we must distinguish between total failure and partial failure. When we use the word it always sounds like total failure when in reality it is not. A total failure is someone who completely misses the very purpose of his existence, why God created him. God alone makes this final judgment. We can't make it because we are so blind and forgetful of the good that we do and the love that we have given.

"Most of us would make the judgment, though, that we are very much partial failures. Each one to differing degrees. A man who has low goals or a few goals may not feel a great sense of failure. While a man who is a dreamer or one who has certain definite unreached goals, that may now seem impossible, may have a feeling of great failure. We can well imagine the same for a man who finds that everything he touches crumbles. There are those who don't try thereby failing, those who try a little and fail, and those who keep on trying and fail.

"But you know what, I think we have failure all wrong. Our greatest failure is misjudging the value of failure and our extreme demoralizing preoccupation with failure. We must learn never to give up. Our greatest glory is that we keep trying. The old sayings, 'true success is to labor' and 'the only man who never makes mistakes is one who never does anything' tell us a lot. Our greatest failure is to give up, lose heart, not to try any more.

"The fourth step on the stairway is, like all the others, basically an attitude. It is an attitude toward our defeats, our shortcomings, our setbacks. These are a fact of life. It is very important how we use these events. It is important what they do to us psychologically. Do they tear us up? Do they dry up our enthusiasm and initiative, take away our fight? If this is the case, then the reality of partial failure is a destructive force. However, let the failures of life urge us on to even greater efforts. Let the temporary defeats of life help us to learn. Let setbacks point out our mistakes and teach us how to approach the problem better the next time. It is then that failure has become a building block leading to greater strength and wisdom.

"Do you now see how vital is your attitude toward failure? Failure is a mixed blessing. It is a temporary setback. 'Every adversity, every failure and heartache carries with it the seed of an equivalent or a greater benefit.'

"Much of our time and energy is wasted in worry and embarrassment over real or imagined failure. We must move toward a new attitude about this reality of life called failure.

"Failure seems to wipe us out. We get very discouraged and quit trying. Failure defeats us. How little we understand. Do you not see that failure is a necessary part of life? Failure is one of the great building blocks of life. Life is not made up of just one inning. The life of a man is made up of many innings. The only one who never fails is the person who is not doing anything, someone who has given up on life, someone who is not climbing the stairway. Most of the time failure hurts our pride but not our character. We should see why we failed in a certain venture and then try to correct our mistakes and, if necessary, change our course of action. There is a wise old Oriental saying that 'our greatest glory is not in never falling but in rising every time we fall.'

"In its most basic sense, to fail means not to accomplish what we set out to do. In this sense, if we are doing anything at all, our lives will be filled with many partial failures. In order to fail we must first strive to accomplish something. Those who are pressing on to reach a goal, those who are following a dream can never be real failures. They are the true conquerers, the true heroes of every age. T.B. Aldric writes, 'They fail, and they alone, who have not striven.' It is hard to count failure as a friend but if you are up and doing, he will be a frequent companion. A companion who should not drag you down but test your character to see if you are really willing to pay the price for success. A daily companion who makes you reevaluate your goals to see if they are really worthwhile. A companion who separates those who really want to succeed from those who just think they do.

"In reality we are not as much a failure as we think. God knows countless good things about us. We forget easily many of our efforts, our good intentions, our numerous good deeds and sacrifices. We remember more easily our mistakes and shortcomings. This over-emphasis in our mind on failure is so unhealthy. We scold more than we praise, we tear down and criticize more than we build up and congratulate. We forget so much of the good that we and others do each day. Thank God that He is our final judge. He is God who sees with love and never misses the totality of our efforts. Concentrate on the good you try to do and let the failures of life mingle with the good you have done to spur you on to even more generous actions.

"Failure is a teacher. It shows us our shortcomings and tells us what areas of our lives we have to develop. A true champion, in any field of life, works not only on his strengths but especially on his weaknesses. Failure keeps us human, it makes us humble. Failure helps us to understand others and to be more sensitive to other people's talents and strivings. The proud and haughty have not learned by their failures. The wise man accepts failure as a most valuable teacher. Its lessons are not to discourage you but to make you look for new ways to do things and through the pain of your failure to greatly appreciate and rejoice in your final victory. The stumblings and setbacks of every undertaking make success taste ever so much sweeter.

"Frequently we judge failures by the wrong measuring stick. We take society and its norms of success and failure as our guide. But often the society in which we live, the culture that surrounds us is Godless, materialistic, full of false values. It would be like the blind leading instead of being led. We have to judge life by our potential and our worthwhile goals in relation to our efforts. No man can judge me a failure until he knows my potential, my goals and my efforts. Look at your measuring stick for life and be sure that it is not 'to keep up with the Joneses,' or to make someone else happy by 'fulfilling their goals.'

"Since most of life is based on our attitude we must start seeing our shortcomings, mistakes and weaknesses as stepping stones to greater achievements. We must acquire the habit of constantly enriching ourselves through our mistakes. If we are not making any mistakes we better take a close look and see if we are doing *anything*. The trouble is, that is the ultimate failure—doing nothing.

"God loves us deeply. He is not spending time viewing our failures. He is encouraging us to keep developing our potential. God's love for us goes way beyond our mistakes. It is a love that draws out the best in us, a love that does not leave us when we fail but says 'I am with you, do not get discouraged, together we will turn your weakness into strength.' Someone once said that 'a saint is a sinner who never quits trying.'

"For some mysterious reason we are lovely in the eyes of God in spite of our failures. He can see that potential, that wonderful person we are becoming. Can you imagine a greater 'failure' than God's son hanging on a criminal's cross? I have worked with people in prison most of my life. Some are there because they have broken the law.

Some are there with a just sentence. There are some who are guiltless, having been falsely accused and sentenced. But whatever the circumstances of any man's life, failure is not the end of the journey but only a step along the way. Enter each day with the uplifting thought that God is with you and that you are going to do your best this day.

"When failure does hit, and it frequently will, our job is to never give up but to keep on trying, to keep on learning from our mistakes. In the game of life we must not waste time trying to be the score keeper, but to remain an active participant.

"My dear friends, William Gladstone wrote 'no man ever becomes great or good except through many and great mistakes.' In 1933, Aldous Huxley wrote some words that give deep insight into the fourth step on the stairway of life, the constructive use of failure. 'Experience is not what happens to a man; it is what a man does with what happens to him.'"

5

Be a Doer

DONELLA LANGE did things in life backward. She was born rich, then she married "poor." You might say she got a late start on her second career, too. After raising a family, she started devoting her mind and energy to organizing things that she thought would give her community a better quality of life. It all started very innocently when she organized a farmers' market, then it grew and grew. Today Town and Country West has not only a farmers' market but a roller skating rink, a small community clinic, twenty-eight quaint little retail shops, a neighborhood theatre and a community swimming pool. Donella still doesn't know how it all happened but as each need arose, a plan was devised to meet the need. More people had jobs and more people had service and recreation in her small mid-western town. Donella Lange's life had been full and happy as a wife and mother, but Town and Country West added to her sense of joy and fulfillment in life.

Frederick Carter had met Donella and her family some years ago and he was anxious to hear her present the next step on the stairway.

Mrs. Lange addressed the group. "One of the joyful experiences of life is to live according to the scriptural passage in St. James exhorting us to be 'doers of the Word and not hearers only, deceiving yourselves.' How many wonderful ideas, good suggestions and worthwhile inspirations have come to our mind and we did nothing about them? How often have others proposed good suggestions and brought to light needed projects and we let the opportunity slip by? What a tragedy that our lives are so conditioned and we are so satisfied to merely hear about something that needs to be done rather than doing it. The world is full of clubs and organizations that meet and talk and then do nothing. The doers of this world have such a great vocation, while those who only hear the word and do nothing have such a horrible judgment. Agreed, this is a difficult step on the stairway. We love to take it easy. We love to ridicule and make fun of the doers. We prefer to hear and not to respond. But your life takes a great turning point when you became a doer.

"Consider the hours of the day. We know that we should spend some time in reflection and planning, if not, our lives would go in circles and we would not be placing first things first. But outside of the regular eight hours on the job, how many of the other sixteen are wasted in idleness and procrastination? Even within the framework of the eight so-called working hours, how much time do we waste? Often we do only what is asked of us or just what the other workers are doing.

"I suppose much of my life has been in the category of hearer only, thereby deceiving myself. I have many wasted hours I am ashamed of and I know that I will have to answer for this misused time. These hours will never return, they will never come back to me. I am not talking about the much needed time to rest, the much needed time for recreation, or the time to plan or just get away for a while. I am talking about the hours, days, weeks and months that I could and should have been working, achieving, being a doer. Being a doer must fit into all the categories of my life and the goals I have set within these categories. Our real problem is, not enough time to do all the things that we should be doing. So it is extremely important to use time wisely.

"I must be a doer in relation to the health and condition of my body. I must be actively growing in my spiritual life. My social life and my obligations to the community must be worked on. I have to be a doer and not a hearer only when it comes to my family life, my vocation, my financial well-being and all my special personal goals in life. We must learn to become doers. We must make this one of the greatest goals of our life.

"Think, each day is a miniature of my life, This very day is a miniature of how I spend my time, whether I am only a hearer or whether I am filling my life with action by trying to get things done. Experience should teach me that I am going to have to find some way to make a doer out of

myself. We find men and women that are doers in
only one area. Take for example a man who works
fairly hard at his job but then neglects his family,
or his spiritual life or his financial affairs. Being a
doer must permeate all categories and areas of my
life.

"What makes a man a doer? Some people seem
to have this quality by their nature and disposi-
tion. Most of us, though, have to make this a prime
target of our lives. We tend to do only what we
have to do. We tend to follow the crowd. We tend
to settle for much less than what God intends for
us. Our creator is constantly inspiring us to keep
developing our potential and we can only do this
by being DOERS.

"Goals are essential. A plan of action is essential. Motivation and attitude are essential. Consist-
ency is most essential. But how do you arrive at
all of these and put them together as a workable
team? How do you become a doer?

"Only one way: Make yourself accountable for
your time. Start slow if you have to. Have just one
project for the morning, one for the afternoon and
one for the evening. When the morning is over,
take account. If you were not a doer, think about
it, pray over it, cry over it, urge yourself on, start
over again. We all have many and sometimes
different reasons for not being doers. It might be
fear of failure, fear of ridicule, laziness, years of
bad work habits or we might think we need certain
crutches before we can work. It could go very deep
into our personality and experiences. So we must
hold ourselves accountable over short periods of
time. Don't become a fanatic, but know that being
a doer is essential if we are to climb the stairway.

Each of us is different but in our own way we must become doers.

"A doer makes himself responsible for his own time. Some people are lost the minute they leave work and have no one to tell them what to do. The rest of their day is a pitiful waste of time. Some people even need someone to show them what to do at work. They have no initiative, imagination or foresight. But the doer makes himself responsible for the minutes of his day, the hours of his life. He knows that time slips by very quickly. He knows how easy it is to waste time. He knows how easy it is to let each precious day of his life float by until it is all gone. What a terrifying realization to suddenly know that your life is coming to a close and you have wasted it. The doer never lets this happen. To him each day is sacred. Time is holy. He knows that he must push himself into action.

"Not only does the doer make himself responsible for his own time, he does not need a boss to manage his time. He becomes very selective in what he is going to do. He studies his abilities and interests. He learns to say a polite but resounding NO to those who try to enmesh him in activities that have little or nothing to do with his goals. A doer is forced to do this because early in life he learns that you can't do everything and please everyone. We waste many hours of life until we learn this lesson. Man has to be selective. He has to have goals and follow them. This is one of the great powers of a doer. By doing, he knows that only so much can be done. The hours in a day are few. We are limited by our health and our talents. No time can be wasted in trying to fulfill someone else's goals. The doer sees this and responds by setting his goals carefully and using his time wisely.

"Was I a doer today? Or did I let excuses hold me back? What excuse did I give? Lack of talent. Sickness. No money. No time. No more excuses, everyday I must make up my mind to get things done. I must start each day with a positive attitude that this will be a day of accomplishment. The needs of the world are great. Men and women are needed who will be doers of the Word and not hearers only.

"Bad habits have settled in over the years. So to succeed I must start holding myself accountable. I must realize more keenly each day that I will only go through this world once. I must start each day with the saying in my heart, 'I shall pass through this world but once. Any good thing I can do, or any kindness that I can show any human being, let me do it now and not defer it. For I shall not pass this way again.' Yes, I will hold myself accountable for my life, I will be a doer.

"Being a doer does not mean that I don't plan, that I don't meditate and have moments of repose, reflection and recreation. Being a doer does mean that my plans and dreams bear fruit, that my ideas move me to action. Being a doer does demand that I have priorities in my life, that what I do is worthwhile. What I do should enrich, ennoble and recreate me. It should be of some service or help to others.

"Since we have only so many hours in a day we must choose wisely what we do. Each day is a part of your lifetime that never returns. The reward of each day is more in the striving than in the victory. The doers of this world may have sweat on their brow, callouses on their hands and criticism in their ear but they have a song in their heart. The song of a good deed well done. The song of accomplishment. The peace of knowing that they tried. A deep sense of fulfillment. The rest they leave in the hands of God, who sees every effort. Doers of the world rejoice, it is the hearers only who have to fear, for they are the ones who deceived themselves. It is the men and women of action, whether by the work of the body, the ideas of the intellect or the spirit of prayer, who make this world a better place in which to live."

6

Thankfulness

MARK DUTTON had been in the war. Not the big war but our intervention in Korea. But it was big enough for him. He came back a quadriplegic, paralyzed in both arms and both legs. Before the fighting Mark had done all the right things. He finished high school with honors, became a master carpenter and married his childhood sweetheart. Then everything seemed to go downhill. But not in Mark's eyes. He knew he had been dealt a hard blow, but he had a secret builder that is found in all great men and women. After his honorable discharge from the service, he did not wallow in self-pity or self-defeat. Within two years he was part owner of a lumber yard. In three more years he was building low-and-medium income homes in the community. He has since bought out his partners in the lumber company and has purchased a hardware store. He could do all these things because he possessed a forgotten quality that is one of the steps on the stairway to successful living. Had he not possessed this inner power he would have been a sullen and sour man. It is a power we must all cultivate if we are going to make any progress in life. Without it we become bitter and hateful men and women. Frederick Carter bade him to speak.

"Life on this earth seems long. Fifty, sixty, seventy years sounds like a long, long time. But as you grow older you will find that the hours turn into days, the days into weeks and months, and the months into years very quickly. Today becomes yesterday so very fast. As time passes, there is another essential quality needed on our climb on the steps of the stairway. It is called thankfulness. A thankful heart is a great heart. A person who constantly sees things to be thankful for has grasped an inner secret of life. He has grasped the sixth step on the stairway.

"With all of its difficulties, hardships, disappointments, setbacks and failures, still every day has so many moments to make us thankful. We must be a thankful person before all else. Every step we take, every breath we breathe, so many sights we see should evoke from our inner being a grateful cry of 'thank you.'

"The person who doesn't have a sense of thankfulness cannot make real progress. He might make or inherit wealth or might become temporarily powerful, but he also will be very shallow and selfish. He will miss the great inner beauty that he is called to and much of life will pass him by.

"Yet many people do not have this essential quality of being truly thankful. It so seldom comes into their daily way of living. They are lacking in a proper vision of what blessed things are happening around them, to them and in them. Much of life comes and goes and they have no sense of the marvel.

"People who can't find anything to be thankful for are in deep trouble. Deep trouble because they have eyes and do not see, ears and do not hear. Great men are brought to their knees daily with a thank you on their lips. One of the truest signs of greatness is being thankful. A person cannot be truly great and lack this quality. And like all qualities, it is partly acquired. Some people, because of their more sensitive nature, acquire the thankfulness habit with greater ease but it is a must for everyone. To see miracles exploding all around us should make a man thankful. To be thankful is to be truthful. To be thankful is to face life as it really is. The person who is not thankful is not great because he misses the very events that would make him great. He just doesn't see them. A thankful heart is preparing to see even more things to be thankful for. Just like the more we exercise any part of our body the stronger it gets, so too the more we practice thankfulness the greater our ability to really see many more reasons to say 'thank you.'

"Once there was a Boy Scout troop that got a special assignment from the Scout Master. Each boy was given a six foot by six foot area to occupy and observe. At first the scout sees next to nothing—only grass and dirt. But he must stay in the prescribed area for at least one hour. As time goes by, his powers of observation grow. Yes, this is a piece of grass but next to it is a weed. A few inches over is another type of grass and a tiny, almost unnoticeable, flower. Here is a stone, there is a pebble and oh, what a variety of insects. Thankfulness is like that. Every time we are thankful we prepare ourselves to see something else to be thankful for.

"A thankful heart draws blessings. Those who are thankful for what they have, receive more. They draw to themselves gifts, treasures and blessings that the unthankful person can hardly imagine. The good Lord notices who appreciates the blessings of life and he showers them with more. The thankful heart acts like a magnet; it draws to itself the choicest blessings this world has to offer. Our greatest blessing is to be a great and good person—a thankful person.

"We can also say that the opposite is true. To have blessings and opportunities and not be thankful for them will decrease our ability to receive. It will decrease our ability to see the wonderful things that are happening to us. The ungrateful man is like a net with a hole in it. He loses many precious objects. Not to notice your blessings, to seldom say thank you deep down within your being is a sure sign that you are a real failure as a human being. That surging feeling of gratitude should become so natural to us that we see an endless stream of events, people, and blessings that make up the happiness of our life.

"Did you ever stop to think that a verbal 'thank you' to a person is a great help in having other people want to help you? The great leaders of this world, whether they be in business, military or whatever their life's work, draw around them people who aid them in their progress because they are able, in many different ways, to say thank you. Greatness is not ashamed to share the praise. Great men and women don't hesitate to be thankful. They see very clearly what others have helped them to achieve. The football halfback appreciates the linemen. The pitcher his fielders. The general his troops. The industrialist his workers and staff. They know that they have not and cannot go it alone. If they want to succeed, they need others. They know that the thanks they feel in their hearts and have on their lips will help guarantee their continued success. We all soften up a bit and want to help out more when someone thanks us. It is also the greatest way in the world to have others want to help us.

"Being thankful changes our personality. It changes it for the better. Man accomplishes much through his personality. If he develops a pleasing and gracious personality he is able to move through life selecting the choicest fruits of his endeavors. If on the steps of the stairway of life we learn to listen, work and be thankful we will reap a rich harvest. The thankful person is constantly changing for the better because he pays tribute to all who help him make progress, thus he is able, with the continued aid of events and people, to make even greater strides. The thankful man is developing a rich personality that gives him an ever-growing sense of being on the right track. He is open to his strengths and weaknesses.

"To be thankful is to use well the blessings that have been given to us. The highest form of thanksgiving is to make use of the gifts we have been given. If someone gives us a dress or suit we should wear it. If we have a good singing voice we should sing. If we have healing hands we should heal. Using our gifts is a sign of thankfulness. How can anyone be really thankful if they only say thank you with their lips and never by their actions? To tithe not only applies to our financial blessings. It applies to all our gifts—of body and mind and affairs. Thankfulness must show itself in deeds.

"The ungrateful and thankless person is always carrying around the heavy debt of not paying tribute to those who have labored for him. Soon he is weighed down in debt. He loses his objectivity and truthfulness. Eventually he completely deludes himself, thinking he is doing it all. He sees neither God nor man. To hear him talk and to listen to his way of thinking, you would imagine he had no parents and never had a teacher. You would suppose he created all animals and caught them for his food. You would think it was he who invented the sunshine, and the fresh air. His personality becomes so self-centered and unrealistic that it is harder and harder for him to get cooperation in his endeavors. He has missed a most important step on the stairway—being thankful.

"There is nothing more beautiful and more encouraging than the thankful person. In being thankful we pave a sure road to greatness. We pave the way to do great things. How could we ever thank enough the great men and women who have written the books we have read? Some of our greatest benefactors are the authors who have lifted us up from defeat and despair to new hope and courage. What great debt of thanks is owed those writers of biographies and autobiographies who have opened up all the joys, sorrows, struggles and victories of the human heart. Who can thank God and man enough for the Holy Bible? From the sunrise in the morning to the small child in his mother's arms an infinite chorus of thanksgiving should be proclaimed.

"Do you have problems and troubles? Say amen and alleluia. For every problem you have I can find someone with a greater one who is using it to praise God and grow in strength and wisdom. God sometimes allows us to be put on our back so that we may look upward. If God is your source and power you will be a thankful person. You will learn to concentrate on your blessings and put your misfortunes to good use. We need a nation of thankful people.

"The greatest stumbling block to a happy and successful life is to be an unthankful person. This would hold you back from everything else. If you can't see blessings—if you can't see your blessings— you must drop everything else and begin to see all over again with your eyes. You cannot walk the stairway without a thankful heart. I thank you Lord for all the blessings you have given me this day. I know that I see only a small part of your blessings, but help me each day to be more thankful and thereby open up my life to other blessings that I never dreamed could be mine. The thankful person can make leaps and bounds on the stairway of life. His life is one continuous reaping of blessings and rewards because he learned how to say 'thank you.' "

Respect

SHE was young, black and we might add, very beautiful. Karen Reese was also a first-rate lawyer. She had worked her way through college and law school by playing the piano and being the lead singer in a local band. But her recent undertakings gave her little time for law or music. Karen had just celebrated her thirty-eighth birthday and she was already fully committed to a different career.

As she practiced law Karen became more and more aware of the need for a newspaper that would relate to the needs and aspirations of her people. She wanted everyone in the community to be aware of what was really happening. Her newspaper was well into its fifth year and she was working on extending its influence beyond her city into the county and even the state. Her eventual dream was to start a national newsletter that would get into the hands of the type of person who could get things done. Karen Reese's ability to relate to people of all ages, backgrounds and needs made her a much sought-after speaker. The step on the stairway she was about to introduce was her favorite topic. With it you can reach the stars; without it you labor in vain. She shuddered at the thought of the small amount of time her host allowed each speaker. The topic was so important. But it was time to unveil the next step on the stairway. Karen began her talk.

"My dear friends, to be a truly successful person you must have a deep respect for yourself and for others. This is the seventh step on the stairway of life.

"I must, first of all, have a deep respect for myself. If I am to 'love my neighbor as myself,' then I must have a proper love of myself. Those who have a low esteem of themselves have a low esteem of others. The thief, the criminal, the hater, the slanderer first lose self-respect, then they lose respect for others. You cannot hurt, destroy, ridicule if you have self-respect.

"Man is made up of two parts. On our journey through life we travel with a body and a soul. Often we emphasize one to the detriment of the other, but to function properly there must be harmony between these two facets of our being. There must be a balance of care and time spent on each. It has been known for a long time that our bodies and souls are intimately connected. But each person must come to a practical realization of this in his daily living. A wholesome spirit has a lot to do with how your body feels and functions. The health of the body is very essential to the productivity of your spirit.

"Respect must show itself in action. If we respect our body, we eat certain foods and leave others aside. We eat only the amount of food our body needs. The respectful person sees to it that his body gets fresh air, sunshine, rest and recreation. Cleanliness is a product of respect. All these things added together give us the strength and endurance to live a full day. Respect for your body pays off in great dividends. Those who have a true respect for their body have a well-mapped out plan for keeping their body healthy and fit. Our bodies are temples through which a spirit works. Our bodies are sacred instruments that deserve our special care.

"The spirit needs the same attention. The books we read, the thoughts we dwell on, the friends we choose, all show respect or a lack of it. Just as we must have a proper love for the body that shows itself in action, so too must we have daily spirit-builders that show true love for our inner life. Placing a high value on the spiritual realities of life is essential to growth and progress. The man who respects the spiritual part of his nature is a man of prayer. He talks with God easily and comfortably. He feels at home in things of the spirit. You can learn much about a man, and see where he stands in his respect for his spirit, by seeing if he prays and how he prays.

"We show respect for ourselves in many ways. The way we dress, talk, think and play. We become the mirror of how we feel about ourselves. Once a person stops tearing himself down and begins to see his worth and value, then he begins to make progress. 'I'm no good.' 'I'll never amount to anything.' 'Why waste your time on me?' These are all sentences expressing a lack of respect for the beautiful person you are. If you think you are no good or worthless, you will become so in your attitudes and actions. Build up respect for yourself. Dream dreams. Make efforts. Never quit trying. God does not make trash and God made you.

"One sign of a growing self-respect is the respect you have for others. You don't really respect yourself if you don't respect other human beings, if you don't respect the world in which you live. Each man's personal belongings are holy. The day you cannot see the sacredness of a man's property and possessions, how will you be able to appreciate the sacredness of his feelings, his reputation, his ideas, his dreams, his culture? Respect never comes unless you sense the sacredness of all life. Respect is based on the sacredness of God's creation and that each person you meet is made in the image and likeness of the creator. A man who steals not only disrespects himself—he disrespects his brothers and sisters. A person who would harm another cares nothing about the brotherhood of man. The greatest value that we can pass on to our children is self-respect and respect for others.

"There are ways that we can cultivate respect. One is to enjoy people. Find ways to make people more interesting to you. Love watching people in action. Enjoy seeing children at play. Marvel at a child in the arms of a mother or father. Allow people on a beach or a crowded city street to fascinate you. View the old and the young in their different moods of life. Rejoice with those who are happy and share the pain with those in sorrow.

Never harbor an attitude that people are stupid or worthless. Always see the best and the most beautiful in those around you. As you let your heart sing with the joyful and cry with those in sorrow, you will be growing. You will be learning to be deeply affected when you see one of your brothers down. You will be learning to celebrate with the human family when it counts its blessings. You will become a part of all that is good and beautiful.

"Respect is a power. It is a power within a person. It is the gift we can give ourselves or share with others. As this power grows it builds the foundation needed for all the other steps on the stairway. It becomes the unifying factor that ties all the other steps together. Don't ever neglect it.

"The person who respects himself and respects others is an honest person. He is truthful and trustworthy. His word is good, you can count on him. He loves the truth however painful it may be. The truth makes him free.

"He is fair. Men in every field of endeavor honor this virtue. You can demand a lot from yourself and from others as long as you are fair. Being fair includes many things—spending time with your family, sharing your part of the load with your co-workers, listening to others with an open mind, paying your workers a living wage, sharing your profits and honoring your commitments. Being fair stems from the respect you have for others.

"Much of our happiness depends on getting along with other people. Everybody has faults and failings but we need other people to help us if we are to succeed. The respect we show for the men and women who are on this journey with us, reflects back and makes us worthy of respect.

"Respect breeds a man of character. Character does not mean only having strong convictions; some of the world's most selfish men certainly had strong convictions. The basis of a strong character comes from being truthful, honest and loving. These three qualities are the building blocks of character. These three are born of respect for self and others.

"Respect must be all-inclusive. You can't pick and choose. There must be respect for all life. Respect for the unborn. Respect for children and the aged. Respect for the single person and for married life. Respect for the dying. As our world becomes more filled with cement and less with flowers, more filled with highrise apartments and less with trees, more filled with noisy machines and less with the song of birds, we must make greater efforts to deepen our respect for people and the world of nature. If we ever lose our sense of the sacred, if we ever lose our sense of respect, then we will have destroyed ourselves and the earth God placed in our hands as its caretakers. Once we lose our sense of respect, then we have lost the light of goodness and greatness that we were to pass on to future generations.

"Marcus Aurelius Antoninus wrote, 'The best way of avenging thyself is not to become like the wrongdoer.' Thus the respectful person lives by creative growth. He is not self-centered but people-centered, and God-centered. The litter on our highways, streets and yards lets us know whether we are respectful or not. Parents teaching their children hatred and mistrust through derogatory stories, remarks and comments toward other races shows if we are a people of respect. Respect or disrespect filters down into all our actions and all our thoughts. The final destroyer of every nation and every civilization is the erosion of respect. When you lose respect, you lose truth; when you lose truth, you have lost freedom. My friends, value nothing higher, champion nothing harder. Endure any sacrifice to be a respectful person. Every successful person, every wonderful family and every great nation had this same basic quality: self-respect and respect for others.''

Self-Motivation

SOME fifteen years ago Larry Alston started a small publishing firm specializing in gift books, greeting cards, posters and limited editions of paintings. Larry was a writer, photographer and painter doing a large amount of the company's creative work himself. From a small work force of Larry Alston and one part-time worker, the company now had twenty-seven full-time employees. Larry's small publishing company was now the size he wanted, leaving him sufficient time both for business and creative pursuits.

The Larry Alston of today is a far cry from the person people knew during his high school and college days. It took a skiing accident to trigger the rebirth of Larry Alston. Two years out of college saw Larry, a talented young man, wasting his time and abilities. A badly broken leg with time to read and think set in motion the change from a life going nowhere to an exciting life with dreams, goals and the challenge of getting things done. Mr. Alston knew that he would be presenting the important last step on the stairway of successful living. He looked forward to sharing with the group the great change that had come over him. A smile of friendship passed between Larry and Mr. Carter. It was time to begin.

"My friends, I am now going to discuss with you the eighth step on the stairway—self-motivation.

"If you want something you will go after it. If you desire something it will eventually be yours. I have yet to see this work. We have a lot to learn about motivation and we use the word in many confusing ways. Many people use the word in the sense of being attracted to something. They feel they want something, or desire something, or it is a part of their dream world. For example, someone will say, 'I wish I weighed 175 pounds.' But is my wish and my desire really motivation? Attraction, desire and want must come first but motivation really means something else. Motivation comes from the Latin verb movere—to move. True motivation means to be moving toward something, not just to be attracted by it. This added element is very important. The motivated person is on the move, he is moving toward the person, the possession or attitude that attracts him.

"What will make us move toward something we want? What will spur us into action to get what we desire? Thousands of people enter goals programs each year. They are told to set goals, listing all the things they want, then to write out a plan of action and to begin working on it. But nothing really happens. They set the goals for the things they want. They write out an elaborate plan of action, listing all the obstacles that have to be overcome and the solutions to these obstacles. Why do they never reach the goal? Usually we can figure out what we want but we can't move ourselves to take the steps necessary for succeeding. What makes a person do the things necessary to get what he wants?

"People do things for one of three reasons, or some combination of the three. The lowest level of motivation but a widely used one is fear. Fear of punishment or other painful consequences. If I don't go to school or church I will be punished. When the outside force of fear is removed we no longer do the thing we did not want to do in the first place. The next level of motivation, and another widely used motivator, is reward. I work only for the pay. Take away the stick holding the carrot in front of the donkey and the animal stops moving. Reward is another valid and widely used motivator. But the highest level of motivation is to be motivated by attitude. This is an inner motivation that does not depend on fear or reward alone. Very few possess it. It is the eighth step on the stairway, which we will call self-motivation, or self-leadership. This type of motivation has an added dimension of power that our mere wants and desires don't have. With self-motivation we are motivated to pay the price. Self-motivation moves us toward leadership. To be a leader is not just to have a goal. To be a leader is to have a goal and to move toward it. True leadership is first and foremost to move yourself. To lead or move others may or may not come. Leadership of others needs those extra ingredients of charisma and being in the right place at the right time, with goals others believe in. But this step on the stairway concerns basically only you. That you are motivated by attitude. That you are a self-starter who is willing to pay the price—these are the ingredients of self-motivation.

"Many courses, books and programs on motivation unintentionally mislead us. They make it sound as though everyone is willing and ready to pay the price to reach their desire. This is a misconception. People may be theoretically capable but most are not even remotely willing to pay the price. It becomes clearer and clearer that many men and women are nowhere close to being self-motivators. Their goals are very weak and this is the way they want it. Not everybody wants to be a self-leader. The great tragedy is that man was created as a being who should constantly keep improving, a being who on reaching one goal sets a higher one. He must always be activating his potential. He is in a state of becoming. Man, through cycles of rest and action, keeps improving himself. Each day is a new challenge to become a better person.

"Now I must ask you to stop and seriously consider if you want to move toward better and better goals. Do you desire to improve and advance? Do you have a dream world of things, positions, powers, abilities and attitudes that you want to acquire? This is important. If you don't have certain desires of the mind, if you don't have a world of dreams, then there is no reason for you to learn the secrets of motivation. If you don't have dreams that you'd like to make real, then there is no need for you to see if you have the capacity to be motivated by attitude, to be motivated to pay the price. Alan Oken writes:

You were born to serve a purpose.
This purpose is what we call your 'mission,'
your reason for being, your Earth-trip.
To find this out is a trip in itself
but it is all a part of growth.
In order to accomplish your true life's work
you must first establish the path by which
you are to reach it.
Everything in life is a step toward
or a vehicle to reach something higher.

"Say that you do have areas in your life where you would like to see change. Let us agree that you do have goals you want to attain. Most of us can sit down, review our lives and set goals. Most people can list the obstacles to these goals and figure out a plan of action to overcome these obstacles. But here is where it stops. The majority of men and women after setting goals, listing obstacles and working out a plan of action then come to an abrupt halt. Oh, there are efforts and accomplishments now and then, but most of the time just a frustrating series of starts and stops. What is missing? Why do many people only get this far? Motivation is the step on the stairway that keeps people making progress. It is the step that keeps us always reaching our goals and setting new ones. Why do so many people fail on this important step?

"Look at motivation again. Study it closely.

The first question is: Do I want to be motivated on the level of action? Am I willing to pay the price of time and effort needed to attain my goals? There is only one way to find out. Test yourself. Take one of your short-range goals, a goal that can be accomplished in a few weeks or a few months. Concentrate on this goal. Like all other powers the ability to motivate yourself takes practice. Write out your short-range goals as clearly as you can. Study the obstacles and put in writing your plan of action to overcome these obstacles. Go over the goal, the obstacles and the plan of accomplishing the goal every day. If you can accomplish this one goal, it is a good sign that you are one of the few who has the guts and determination to be self-motivated. Yes, one of the very few. You will now have the confidence and the growing ability to tackle other short-range goals and eventually start working on long-range goals, goals that take more than six months, maybe even years, to accomplish. But what happened? How did you do it? You must have had what we might call the ingredients that bring motivation into play. You had desires. You had dreams. You wanted certain things. Few of us are 'born' dreamers and goal setters. A power from the outside touches our life. Our parents, family or friends motivate us. A good book inspires us. A great teacher wakes us up. Usually the key to motivation is our environment, our self-image, our sensitivity. So some people have a great head start. Others have to reach down to touch the bottom and improve many outside influences if they are to succeed.

"But remember, my friends, we get nowhere if the dream stays only in our mind, or on a piece of paper. For true success your goal must become interiorly important to you, you must become a self-motivator. You must do things not because your parents want you to, or your wife wants you to, or your friends want you to, or the author of a book wants you to, or your minister wants you to, but because YOU want to and you know that what you are doing is right. This begins to happen when you look at your goal, search deep down within yourself and then are able to say I WILL PAY THE PRICE EVERY DAY. If you can't say that, it is not one of your real goals; forget about it. Look at the words closely. PAY THE PRICE (you are willing to give something in exchange for the goal) and EVERY DAY (not hit or miss).

"You must find out the cost of the goal. You must ask yourself if the goal means enough to you that you are willing to pay the price. If your answer is yes, then you will move into action. A self-motivated person is someone who lines up his actions with his dreams. The type of motivation that bears results is the inner motivation that makes you want something so much that you are willing to work for it. All levels of motivation are important, but only self-motivation leads to leadership and success.

"Let me speak for a moment on an aspect of motivation that is most essential and seldom talked about. The highest levels of self-motivation can only be achieved by the person who is trying to draw closer to God, the person who is striving for goodness of life and closeness to the will of God.

"The person who wants to reach and maintain a high degree of self-motivation is working in an area that often surpasses his limited strength. He is trying to live in the realm of a positive mental attitude, super will power and a creative imagination. Because of this he is going to have to acquire certain powers of the spirit. He will need God's help in the beginning and all along the way.

"Before I share the three special powers you need to gain the ability to be a good self-motivator, let me first reveal how you can acquire these powers.

"How do we place ourselves in a position to benefit from God's loving care and assistance? God's love, care and help are always present, so the real question is: how can we gradually prepare ourselves to receive God's constant shower of love and help? The flow of God's aid and love is ever constant. He wills only what is good for us and He is always interested in our progress. The benefits are always there, so why do we not gather them in and begin to develop the great power of self-motivation?

"The answer is that our efforts at prayer are weak and haphazard. We don't communicate with God. We don't open up to receive His gifts and help. We seldom find out His beautiful plans for us and thus we lose out on those very important powers we desperately need to be truly successful as self-motivators.

"To make life a successful journey, be a prayerful person. Become finely turned to God's will. Prayer brings you the daily courage and perseverance you need. It teaches you how to be thankful, how to handle mistakes, how to say 'I am sorry.' Without prayer you enter into a circular pathway that winds its way downward ending in mediocrity and failure. With prayer a person takes an upward path that rises above petty selfishness and produces a personality geared for true success. Prayer lets you know when it is time to take the next step on the stairway.

"Prayer prepares you for the successes that come with every victory. It has a calming effect that lets wisdom shine through, revealing the true values of life. It helps you to set worthwhile goals. Prayer ushers you into each new stage of your life and enables you to handle your achievements and make stepping stones out of your failures. If you are not a person who prays, your efforts at self-motivation will not last long. They will crumble with the first winds of adversity.

"What then are the three special powers that we need for a high level of self-motivation that can only be obtained through frequent prayer?

"The first great power that we need, is a superabundance of perseverance. We are going to encounter many obstacles, failures and discouragements. Many of our goals will be achieved only after years of striving. We would give up in our efforts at self-motivation if we did not have the courage and power to persevere. God grants this power to us through prayer.

"The second great power that we need is the ability to set good and honorable goals—goals that will enrich and not weaken, goals that are creative and not destructive. Our goals must lead us toward being better people. Without prayer this is impossible. We become too self-centered, too falsely ambitious, too prone to hurt others on our way to the top. Prayer teaches us how to formulate good goals and how to reach them without hurting others.

"The third great power—the strength to be humble—we need because of what can happen to us after we reach our goals. We are not prepared for success. We can't handle it. We become vain, proud and conceited. We lie back and waste our success or we begin to hoard our blessings. A daily program of prayer prepares us for the success that we will achieve as each of our goals becomes a reality. Prayer enables us to realize that we did not succeed alone but had help all along the way. Prayer periods enable us to set other good goals to replace those accomplished. The needs of victory are as great as the needs of defeat.

"Oh, what a wonderful lifelong adventure! To live by attitude. To work each day at being a self-motivator. This is the truest of freedoms and the greatest of accomplishments."

The Treasure

THE large grandfather clock had just finished striking the last stroke of midnight. A new day was beginning, the Lord's day. Each speaker had briefly laid out the treasure—the eight steps necessary for successful living. Instead of being tired the participants were wide awake with excitement and joy. Each guest had presented only one key idea of each step and the support and closeness that this meeting had brought about flowed through all the members.

Frederick Carter's face was flushed from the excitement of the last four hours. He tried to force himself to speak slowly but again and again the emotion of the past evening showed in his voice.

"Ladies and gentlemen, make the day the mirror of the week, make the week the mirror of the month and make each month the mirror of your year. Each one of you has sown good seed on good ground. Now the ground and the seed have become one. We are the treasure.

"Most people studying success books, motivation courses and inspirational literature are hoping to acquire things. A better job, a newer home, a more expensive car. But we are the final product of the eight steps, we are the treasure. All things are secondary to that. We become the treasure. If not, all has been a waste of time. All the material things that come our way are not the main treasure. You are the treasure. No thing outside you can be as valuable as you. You didn't just stumble onto the great treasures of life, or find them by accident. You found them because you were searching for them. The easy shortcuts to success lead nowhere. Each step on the stairway looks so obvious and so easy, yet day after day we journey past them without noticing their value. They are deceptive. What looks obvious must be found. What looks easy must be worked for.

"The person who has a material treasure has to be bigger than that treasure or it will destroy him. If he does not become the main treasure he will not know how to properly use what he has acquired. If it is bigger than he it will only bring misery and unhappiness. All success depends on your becoming the treasure.

"You are the treasure. Your body will have health, strength and endurance. The eight steps will clear your mind and help you to seek fresh air, nutritious food and the proper amount of exercise. Your body is an intimate companion and many of your goals for success are concerned with its well-being.

"You are the treasure. Your soul, your will, and your intellect will be filled with good thoughts and a generous spirit. Good books, wholesome ideas and uplifting friends will be your companions. Prayer will draw you close to God by issuing forth a deep faith, hope and love. These three produce a life of good works. The steps on the stairway enrich your soul. You now have an inner strength of character that no storm or tempest can defeat. Your attitude of joy and perseverance makes you unbeatable. You see the present struggle but you also see the future victory because you are strong in the spirit.

"You are the treasure. Your social and community life are always a rewarding experience because your inner beauty reaches out and touches your recreation and community involvement. The steps of the stairway have taught you how to become a living spring that does not run dry. It is constantly being replenished because it reaches out to share. You have received that you might give and your giving has enabled you to always keep receiving. Your social and community life is not drained by trying to 'keep up with the Joneses,' but is always full of a rewarding sense of accomplishment because you absorb from the good, learn from the evil and help the less fortunate.

"You are the treasure. In your vocation of life, whether married or single, and the work you do, you enrich yourself by doing everything well. The hours of work are spent in learning and doing the best job possible. The frustrations of work enrich you with patience and perseverance. Even more important, you build a family life that brings a deep satisfaction and happiness. You devote yourself to the happiness of your wife and children, sharing with them the steps of the stairway. Your greatest and most creative work is the time and love and happiness that comes from your vocation as father or mother, husband or wife, brother or sister. All the money, position, power or good that might come from your job cannot compare to it.

"You are the treasure. Your special projects and hobbies enrich you even more. It may be photography, learning a language, carpentry, travel or a multitude of other special enrichers. But you remain the treasure. They are not time wasters, they are self-enrichers. They lead to a wonderful sense of fulfillment and pleasure.

"Yes, you are the treasure. Good intends you to be the treasure by following the eight steps of the stairway. Any material possessions that come to you from learning the secrets of the eight steps are your servants and not your masters. The crowning glory of the mysteries that have been revealed to you is that God is making *you* the treasure that he loves, and not what you acquire or the position of authority you may attain. My friends, you are the end product of the journey up the steps of the stairway."

Mr. Carter turned and looked at the one man in the room who had not yet spoken.

The Plan

PAUL OSHA had not missed a word of the precious speakers. He knew that he was in some way a part of this fascinating meeting, but his role was not yet completely clear. Paul was the second-generation owner of one of the finest book publishing companies in North America. He was in his mid-forties but already, like his father before him, a great publisher of quality books. His sales organization and aggressive methods of distribution gave the books he published an international audience. Paul Osha was thrilled at the presentation of the eight steps on the stairway to successful living, but he knew that most of the speakers were not professional writers. Frederick Carter must want him to publish a book. But how did Mr. Carter want this done?

"Paul," Mr. Carter said, "I think you know why I have invited you to this meeting. You own a well-established publishing firm that does quality work and has a worldwide network for getting your books distributed. I want you to have the ideas of this meeting written, edited, published and distributed, following certain stipulations. I am going to will all the interest from my monies to this project. Will you undertake the project I have outlined?" The attention of everyone in the room was riveted to the two men.

"Frederick, as you know, I am not a subsidy publishing house. I have never entered into an agreement like this before. What you seem to be asking is that you pay to have this book published and placed on the bookshelves of the world. Is this what you are asking of me?"

The old man let a flicker of a smile cross his face. "Yes, Paul, that and more. I will set up a trust, this year, the interest from which will be used to support this project. Upon my death the executors of my will will have all my wealth placed in the trust. But the stipulations of my plan are very important to me and what I am going to say now is an integral part of what I am asking you to do." The old man's words were spoken softly and deliberately. "It is true that I am asking you to have professional writers, masters of the art of communication, to interview my eight speakers and to compose a book containing the eight essential steps on the stairway of life. But, Paul, how the book is distributed is also very important to me. I want it never to go out of print and to always be available, but I don't want all the books to be given away.

"At times a sorrow comes over me when I look back and realize how many years went by before the steps on the stairway were made known to me. I started the climb late in life. Many people and many experiences were needed to bring the steps into my life. So I learned the truth that even though we need the steps as early as possible in life, they often do not appear until our later years. The steps become evident to different people at different stages in life. The book, Paul, must be kept in print and must be kept available. The interest from the money that I have accumulated during my life must be used to keep the *Steps on the Stairway* in bookstores in every country of the world. Thus some of the money must be used for translations. But, Paul, each year some books must be donated to libraries. Each year some books should be donated to teachers, and counselors, especially in the poorer school districts. Each year some books should be donated to community centers and recreation centers. I want the book to be available to those who want to read it."

"Frederick, let me ask a question," Paul said. "I know of your great wealth so why not give away so many books each year, it would be simpler."

"Yes, Paul, it would be simpler but it would violate a great principle of life. Namely, 'when the student is ready the teacher will appear.' Paul, what happens to most of us in life is that we are not ready for the riches that are offered us. Often a man has to go through a certain amount of experiences before he is ready. Suffering, defeat, loneliness often must proceed before we can accept and use wisely what God wants to teach us. You are blessed if you are ready when you are young. To

those pupils who seem ready, a teacher or counselor can offer the book. But many of us are not
ready until later in life. The book must stay available in bookstores, libraries, hospitals, prisons and
military bases around the world. When a person is
ready, I want the book to be there."

"Frederick Carter, what you have presented to
me this Easter Sunday morning has introduced
me to a new life. I can feel this plan is from God
and I want to be part of it. I have learned so much
these past hours that I would consider it a great
honor to publish and distribute *Steps on the Stairway*. The men and women I have met here have
greatly enriched my life. Frederick, the material
blessings that you are giving to this endeavor could
not be used more wisely or more fruitfully."

It was clear that Mr. Carter was deeply touched
by Paul Osha's remarks. Frederick turned to the
eight speakers. "I can never thank you enough for
the part you have played in these sacred events. As
you know, this is my last will and testament. But
what you are doing is much greater than I. You
are passing on to countless members of the human
family one of God's greatest gifts. The steps have
always been there. You are now making them better known, revealing their priceless value. Our days
together and your warm friendship will always
remain most precious. Let us now bid goodbye
and continue our climb up the stairway of life."

A Farewell

YOU have just read the incredible story *Steps on the Stairway*. The stairway is standing before you.

Are you ready to climb? I hope so. Our whole life depends on climbing this stairway. Climbing the stairway will make you a wonderful person. And isn't that what life is all about?

May God bless you.

RALPH RANSOM

ABOUT THE AUTHOR

RALPH RANSOM has lived in Maryland, Washington, D.C., and Louisiana. He is currently living in San Antonio, Texas.

Heartwarming Books
of
Faith and Inspiration

☐	23196	**STEPS ON THE STAIRWAY** R. Ransom	$2.95
☐	22739	**CONFESSIONS OF A HAPPY CHRISTIAN** Zig Ziglar	$2.75
☐	20571	**THE SCREWTAPE LETTERS** C. S. Lewis	$1.95
☐	23069	**A SEVERE MERCY** Sheldon Vanauken	$3.50
☐	20831	**THE GUIDEPOSTS TREASURY OF LOVE**	$2.95
☐	23255	**GUIDEPOST'S TREASURY OF FAITH**	$3.50
☐	20808	**THREE STEPS FORWARD TWO STEPS BACK** Charles S. Swindoll	$2.50
☐	20564	**MEETING GOD AT EVERY TURN** Catherine Marshall	$2.95
☐	20376	**CROSSROADS** by L. Jaworski/D. Schneider	$2.95
☐	14725	**PILGRIMS REGRESS** C. S. Lewis	$2.50
☐	20464	**LOVE AND LIVING** Thomas Merton	$3.50
☐	23277	**POSITIVE PRAYERS FOR POWER-FILLED** **LIVING** Robert H. Schuller	$2.95
☐	14732	**HOW CAN I FIND YOU, GOD?** Marjorie Holmes	$2.50
☐	23614	**THE GREATEST SECRET IN THE WORLD** Og Mandino	$2.95
☐	22638	**THE GREATEST SECRET IN THE WORLD** Og Mandino	$2.75
☐	23404	**CHRIST COMMISSION** Og Mandino	$2.95
☐	20102	**THE 1980'S COUNTDOWN TO** **ARMAGEDDON** Hal Lindsey	$2.95
☐	23268	**I'VE GOT TO TALK TO SOMEBODY, GOD** Marjorie Holmes	$2.95
☐	22805	**BORN AGAIN** Charles Colson	$3.50
☐	23539	**A GRIEF OBSERVED** C. S. Lewis	$2.95
☐	23166	**WITH GOD ALL THINGS ARE POSSIBLE—** Life Fellowship Study	$2.95

Buy them at your local bookstore or use this handy coupon for ordering:

BANTAM NEW AGE BOOKS

Bantam New Age Books are for all those interested in reflecting on life today and life as it may be in the future. This important new imprint features stimulating works in fields from biology and psychology to philosophy and the new physics.

☐	22689	**CREATIVE VISUALIZATION** Shatki Gawain	$3.50
☐	22511	**NEW RULES: SEARCHING FOR SELF-FULFILLMENT** **IN A WORLD TURNED UPSIDE DOWN** Daniel Yankelovich	$3.95
☐	22510	**ZEN IN THE MARTIAL ARTS** J. Hyams	$2.95
☐	20650	**STRESS AND THE ART OF BIOFEEDBACK** Barbara Brown	$3.95
☐	14131	**THE FIRST THREE MINUTES** Steven Weinberg	$2.95
☐	20059	**MAGICAL CHILD** Joseph Chilton Pearce	$3.95
☐	22786	**MIND AND NATURE:** A Necessary Unity Gregory Bateson	$3.95
☐	20322	**HEALTH FOR THE WHOLE PERSON** James Gordon	$3.95
☐	20708	**ZEN/MOTORCYCLE MAINTENANCE** Robert Pirsig	$3.95
☐	20693	**THE WAY OF THE SHAMAN** Michael Hamer	$3.95
☐	23100	**TO HAVE OR TO BE** Fromm	$3.50
☐	23125	**FOCUSING** Eugene Gendlin	$3.95
☐	13972	**LIVES OF A CELL** Lewis Thomas	$2.95
☐	14912	**KISS SLEEPING BEAUTY GOODBYE** M. Kolbenschlag	$3.95

Buy them at your bookstore or use this handy coupon for ordering: